Bear Hugs® for Welcoming Children

Positive activities that make children feel at ease in the classroom

By Patty Claycomb

Illustrated by Marion Hopping Ekberg

Warren Publishing House

Everett, Washington

We wish to thank Marie Wheeler, Tacoma, WA, for contributing the We're So Glad You've Come to School activity in this book.

Editorial Staff
Managing Editor: Kathleen Cubley
Contributing Editors: Kate Ffolliott, Susan Hodges, Elizabeth McKinnon, Jean Warren
Copy Editor: Mae Rhodes
Proofreader: Kris Fulsaas

Design and Production Staff
Art Managers: Uma Kukathas, Jill Lustig
Book Design/Layout: Carol DeBolt, Sarah Ness
Cover Design: Brenda Mann Harrison
Digital Coloring: Sarah Ness
Cover Illustration: Marion Hopping Ekberg
Bear Hugs Logo: Susan Dahlman
Production Manager: Jo Anna Brock

ISBN 1-57029-041-5

Printed in the United States of America
Published by: Warren Publishing House
P.O. Box 2250
Everett, WA 98203

20 19 18 17 16 15 14 13 12 11 10 9 8 7 6 5 4 3 2 1

Introduction

Starting school can be a scary and uncertain time for young children. New faces, new rules, and new rooms can make a young child feel alone and afraid. That's why welcoming children and making them feel comfortable and relaxed is so important. Once that is accomplished, play and learning will soon follow.

But how do you make them feel comfortable? The activities in this book make welcoming children fun and easy. From ideas for the beginning of school, to everyday greeting activities, to special greetings for new children and visitors, you'll find lots of ways to help your children feel like school is a great place to be.

Like the other books in the Bear Hugs series, *Bear Hugs for Welcoming Children* provides you with simple, positive ideas that your children will love. Creating a warm, welcoming environment in your class gets everyone off to a great start.

A
B C
Will

Contents

Welcome Badge

Let your children know you are glad to see them with this Bear Hug.

Materials: Stickers, one for each child; a long block.

Preparation: Place a corner of each sticker around the edges of the block.

Activity: Have your children sit in a circle. Place the sticker block in the middle. Explain to your children that each sticker is a Welcome Badge to welcome them to school. Sing the following song for one of your children, substituting his or her name for *Tyler.* As the child's name is sung, have him or her get up and select a sticker from the block. Repeat the song for each child.

Sung to: "London Bridge"

Someone came to school today,
School today, school today.
Someone came to school today,
And Tyler is his name.

Come and get a Welcome Badge,
Welcome Badge, Welcome Badge.
Come and get a Welcome Badge.
We're glad you came.

Jean Warren

Hint: Surprise your children throughout the year by playing this game periodically. You may wish to use seasonal stickers or stickers that relate to a theme your children are studying.

Welcome Spin

Try this action game to help your children feel welcome in the classroom.

Materials: Plastic 2-liter bottle.

Preparation: None.

Activity: Have your children sit in a circle. Place the bottle in the middle of the circle on the floor. Have the children clap along while you say the following rhyme.

Get to school, open the door,
Take off your coat, sit on the floor.

We'll play a game, we'll have some fun,
We'll spin the bottle, one by one.

We'll welcome all your friends today
While the spinning game we play.

Jean Warren

Choose a child to be the Welcome Spinner. Let the child spin the bottle. When the bottle stops, have the child to whom the bottle is pointing say his or her name. Have everyone say "Good Morning" (or "Good Afternoon") to the child. Then let that child be the new Welcome Spinner. Continue until everyone has been welcomed.

Mother Rabbit

This fun and furry Bear Hug makes welcoming children easy.

Materials: None.

Preparation: None.

Activity: Have your children stand in a circle. Pretend to be a mother rabbit and ask your children to pretend to be your baby bunnies. Sing the following song and have the baby bunnies act out the movements described.

Sung to: "Mary Had a Little Lamb"

Little bunnies hop around,
Hop around, hop around.
Little bunnies hop around,
Make a circle, then sit down.

Little bunnies wave your ears,
Wave your ears, wave your ears.
Little bunnies wave your ears.
I'm so glad you're here.

Little bunnies tap your toes,
Tap your toes, tap your toes.
Little bunnies tap your toes.
If you're happy, wiggle your nose.

I'm so glad you're here today,
Here today, here today.
I'm so glad you're here today.
Now it's time to play.

Patty Claycomb

Dismiss your bunnies one at a time to go and play.

Schoolhouse

This Bear Hug will encourage a welcome feeling any day of the week.

Materials: White posterboard; felt tip markers; tape; small photograph of each child.

Preparation: On the sheet of posterboard, draw a large schoolhouse with a door. Tape it on a wall or a bulletin board at your children's eye level. Put a loop of tape on the back of each child's photograph and place it on the wall or on a table near the posterboard.

Activity: Sit with your children near the schoolhouse drawing. Tell them that the schoolhouse is empty and sad because all the children are gone. Ask them where all the children are. Choose a child to go to school first. Have the child find his or her photo, and then knock on the door of the schoolhouse drawing. Welcome the child to "school" and have him or her place the photo anywhere in the schoolhouse. Continue until each child has been welcomed.

Paper Song

Welcome your children with this Bear Hug song and watch the happy smiles.

Materials: 3-foot length of butcher paper; felt tip markers; tape.

Preparation: Using a felt tip marker, divide the butcher paper into six equal sections. Draw a sun in the first section, raindrops in the second, a train in the third, a bunny in the fourth, a bug in the fifth, and a rug in the sixth. Tape the paper to a wall at your children's eye level.

Activity: Sing the following song to your children. As each item is named, point to its picture on the butcher paper.

Sung to: "Skip to My Lou"

I welcome you as bright as the sun,
I welcome you as quiet as the rain,
I welcome you as loud as a train,
I welcome you each day.

I welcome you as soft as a bunny,
I welcome you as cute as a bug,
I welcome you to sit on the rug,
I welcome you each day.

Patty Claycomb

As your children become more familiar with this song, sing just the "I welcome you" part and let them finish each line. Have them take turns pointing to the appropriate sections on the paper, if desired.

Extension: Place the paper on a table and let your children add their own sun, rain, train, bunny, bug, and rug drawings to the different sections. Or set out magazine pictures of those items for the children to glue in the appropriate places.

Night Smiles

Your children will feel welcome and glad to be at school with this Bear Hug.

Materials: Yellow paper; scissors; black felt tip marker.

Preparation: For each child, cut a 2-inch circle out of the yellow paper. Draw a happy face on each circle. Hide the circles around the room.

Activity: Have the children gather near you. Darken the room. Ask the children to lie on the floor and pretend to sleep. While they are lying still, say the following rhyme.

> **In the middle of the night,**
> **When you think of school**
> **And everyone saying,**
> **"Remember the rules,"**
> **Just think of your teacher**
> **Who welcomes you**
> **And wears a smile**
> **That's just for you.**
>
> *Patty Claycomb*

Now have everyone quietly wake up and search for a happy face while the lights are still dim. Explain that these happy faces are just like your smiling face when you see them at school. Have everyone take their teacher's smile back to their beds. Now lighten the room and wake up the children. Let them take their happy faces home to remind them of how welcome they are.

Get Up and Go

Use this Bear Hug to help your children feel welcome, especially if they are having separation anxiety.

Materials: None.

Preparation: None.

Activity: Say the following poem while your children act out the movements described.

When you wake up in the morning
(Close, then open eyes.)
And you're tired and slow,
(Stretch.)
And you don't want to get up
And go, go, go—
(Shake head.)
Have you ever thought of what to do?
(Put finger on side of head.)
You think of your teacher smiling at you!
(Smile.)

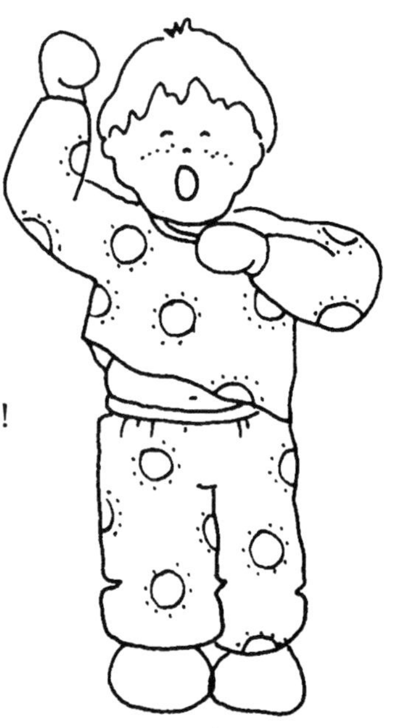

When you wake up in the morning
(Close, then open eyes.)
And you're tired and slow,
(Stretch.)
And you don't want to get up
And go, go, go—
(Shake head.)
Have you ever thought of what to do?
(Put finger on side of head.)
You think of your teacher who cares about you!
(Hug self.)

When you wake up in the morning
(Close, then open eyes.)
And you're tired and slow,
(Stretch.)
And you don't want to get up
And go, go, go—
(Shake head.)
Have you ever thought of what to do?
(Put finger on side of head.)
You think of the fun that is waiting for you!
(Hold out arms and smile.)

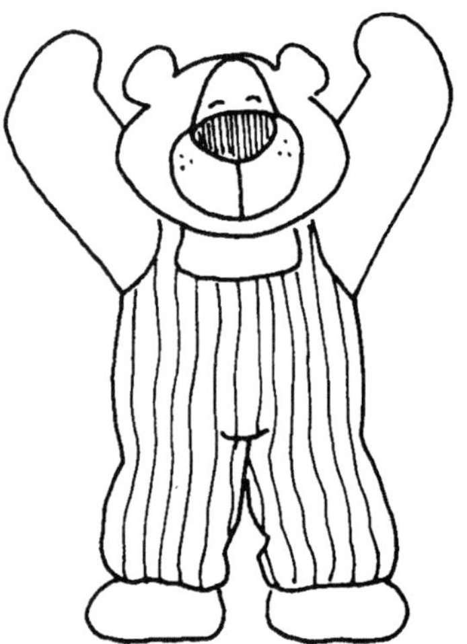

Patty Claycomb

A Rolling Welcome

Roll a welcome to your children with this Bear Hug.

Materials: Rubber ball.

Preparation: None.

Activity: Have your children stand or sit in a circle. Roll a ball to one of the children while you say the following rhyme, substituting the child's name for *Meghan*.

Rolling, rolling, rolling,
We welcome Meghan today.
Rolling, rolling, rolling,
We're glad you came to play.

Jean Warren

Now let the child with the ball roll it to another child while you say the rhyme again. Repeat until each child has had a turn receiving and rolling the ball.

We're So Glad You've Come to School

Welcome your children with this active Bear Hug.

Materials: None.

Preparation: None.

Activity: Have your children sit in a circle. Sing the following song, substituting your children's names for those in the song. Have them listen carefully for their names. As each child hears his or her name, have that child do the motion indicated. Repeat the song until each child has had a turn.

Sung to: "If You're Happy and You Know It"

We're so glad you've come to school today.
We're so glad you've come to school today.
Cameron won't you stand
And shake Gina's hand?
Now everybody clap and say olé!

We're so glad you've come to school today.
We're so glad you've come to school today.
Ellen stamp your feet,
And Maddy smile so sweet.
Now everybody clap and say olé!

We're so glad you've come to school today.
We're so glad you've come to school today.
Jessie take a bow,
And Peter blink right now.
Now everybody clap and say olé!

We're so glad you've come to school today.
We're so glad you've come to school today.
Amanda hop about,
And Luis give a shout.
Now everybody clap and say olé!

We're so glad you've come to school today.
We're so glad you've come to school today.
Roberta touch your chin,
And Bradley show a grin.
Now everybody clap and say olé!

Marie Wheeler

Welcome Moves

Welcome your children with this friendly Bear Hug.

Materials: None.

Preparation: None.

Activity: Have your children stand in a circle. Sing the following song. At the end of the song, have the children sit down and clap their hands.

Sung to: "The Eensy, Weensy Spider"

Good morning on this Monday.
Hello, how are you?
I'm happy that you're here,
And that you came to school.
If you'd like to make
Some Welcome Moves today,
Just sit right down and clap your hands—
I'll know you want to play.

Patty Claycomb

Ask one child to think of a move everyone could do to welcome one another to class. For example, everyone could wave hello, shake hands, hug, or say "Hi!" Continue with as many Welcome Moves as you wish.

Monkey Business

Welcome back a child who has been absent with this Bear Hug.

Materials: None.

Preparation: None.

Activity: Have the child who was absent sit beside you. Help your children recite the following rhyme. At the end of the rhyme have all the children act like monkeys.

Monkeys, monkeys in the zoo
Play around like me and you.

When their friends are not around,
They feel sad and wear a frown.

When their friends come back to play,
They jump and twirl and swing and sway.

So like the monkeys in the zoo,
We would like to welcome you.

Patty Claycomb

Variation: Have a stuffed monkey in the classroom. Let the child who was absent hold it while the rhyme is being said.

Happy Mural

This Bear Hug will help make a child feel welcome if he or she has been absent for a long time.

Materials: 4-foot length of butcher paper; felt tip markers.

Preparation: Place the butcher paper on a table or on the floor, or hang it at your children's eye level on a wall.

Activity: While the child is still absent, make this special mural for him or her. Ask two or three children at a time to draw happy faces on the butcher paper. When the absent child returns, give him or her the paper covered with happy faces. Tell the child that everyone is happy to have him or her back. Let the child add his or her own happy face to the mural before taking it home.

Variation: Instead of drawing happy faces, let your children draw eyes to show that everyone is glad to see the absent child, or trace around hands to show that everyone missed playing with him or her.

The Vacation Rhyme

Welcome back a child who has been gone on an extended vacation with this Bear Hug.

Materials: None.

Preparation: None.

Activity: Sit in a circle with your children. Have the child who was on vacation sit in the middle of the circle or beside you. Say the following rhyme, pausing after each of the first four lines to allow the child to answer the question.

One, one, did you have fun?
Two, two, what did you do?
Three, three, what did you see?
Four, four, can you tell us more?
Five, five, here's a big surprise—
Welcome back!

Patty Claycomb

Have all the children clap and say "Welcome back" to the returning child.

Back at School

Use this Bear Hug to welcome children back from a school vacation.

Materials: None.

Preparation: None.

Activity: Have your children sit in a circle. Sing the following song.

Sung to: "When Johnny Comes Marching Home"

Everyone's back at school today, hurray, hurray!
Everyone's back at school today, hurray, hurray!
Oh, please, oh, please, won't everyone say
What they did while they were away?
Oh, we're all so glad we're back at school today.

Jean Warren

One at a time, let each child tell one thing he or she did on vacation.

Variation: Have your children draw pictures of their vacation activities. Let them hold up the pictures while you sing the song. Then have them name the activities shown in their drawings.

Knock, Knock

Use this Bear Hug to welcome a new child to your room.

Materials: None.

Preparation: None.

Activity: Introduce the new child to your class. Say the following rhyme, substituting his or her name for *George,* and have everyone act out the motions.

Knock, knock.
(Pretend to knock on door.)
Who's there?
(Cup hand behind ear.)
A friend to sing with me.
(Point to self.)

Knock, knock.
(Pretend to knock on door.)
Who's there?
(Cup hand behind ear.)
A friend to play with me.
(Point to self.)

Knock, knock,
(Pretend to knock on door.)
It's George,
Joining us today.

Open the door,
(Open arms.)
Close the door.
(Shut arms.)
Welcome to our day!
(Smile.)

Patty Claycomb

Welcome to Our Class

Welcome a new child or a visitor to your class with this special Bear Hug.

Materials: None.

Preparation: None.

Activity: Have the new child or visitor sit beside you. Have your children sit in a circle. Sing the following song, substituting the names of your children for those in the song. As each child hears his or her name, have the child wave to the person beside you. Continue singing the song until each child has had a chance to wave.

Sung to: "Skip to My Lou"

How do you do? My name is Libby.
How do you do? My name is Kayla.
How do you do? My name is Wayne.
How do you do today?

Gayle Bittinger

TEACHER RESOURCES

1001 SERIES

These super reference books are filled with just the right solution, prop, or poem to get your projects going. Creative, inexpensive ideas await you!

1001 Teaching Props
The ultimate how-to prop book to plan projects and equip discovery centers. Comprehensive materials index lets you create projects with recyclable materials. 248 pp.
WPH 1501

1001 Teaching Tips
Shortcuts to success for busy teachers on limited budgets. Curriculum, room, and special times tips—even a subject index. 208 pp.
WPH 1502

1001 Rhymes & Fingerplays
A complete language resource for parents and teachers! Rhymes for all occasions, plus poems about self-esteem, families, special needs, and more. 312 pp.
WPH 1503

BEAR HUGS® SERIES

This unique series uses a positive approach for dealing with potential problem times. Great ideas for handling specific group situations. Each 24 pp.

Remembering the Rules
These simple rule reminders are fun and nonthreatening.
WPH 2501

Staying in Line
Make staying in line fun, quiet, and safe.
WPH 2502

Circle Time
Get children interested and involved in circle time.
WPH 2503

Transition Times
Help children smoothly shift focus from one activity to another.
WPH 2504

Time Out
Encourage reflective and therapeutic time outs that get results!
WPH 2505

Saying Goodbye
Ease separation anxiety with simple activities and gentle distractions.
WPH 2506

Nap Time
Guide reluctant children into quiet, restful moods.
WPH 2509

Meals and Snacks
Quiet young ones so they can eat without dampening their spirits.
WPH 2507

Cleanup
Encourage cooperation and speedy work with fun cleanup times.
WPH 2508

1•2•3 SERIES

These books present simple, hands-on activities that reflect Totline's commitment to providing open-ended, age-appropriate, cooperative, and no-lose experiences for working with preschool children.

1•2•3 Art *Open-ended Art*
160 pages of art activities emphasize the creative process. All 238 activities use inexpensive, readily available materials. 160 pp.
WPH 0401

1•2•3 Colors
Hundreds of activities for Color Days, including art, learning games, language, science, movement, music, and snacks. 160 pp.
WPH 0403

1•2•3 Books
More than 20 simple concept books to make, including sequences, textures, and weather. 80 pp.
WPH 0406

1•2•3 Murals *Cooperative Art*
More than 50 simple murals to make from children's open-ended art. 80 pp.
WPH 0405

1•2•3 Reading & Writing
250 meaningful and non-threatening activities to develop pre-reading and pre-writing skills. 160 pp.
WPH 0407

1•2•3 Rhymes, Stories & Songs *Open-ended Language*
Open-ended rhymes, stories, and songs for young children. 80 pp.
WPH 0408

NEW! 1•2•3 Shapes
Hundreds of activities for exploring the concept of shapes—circles, squares, triangles, rectangles, ovals, diamonds, hearts, and stars. 160 pp.
WPH 0411

1•2•3 Math
Hands-on activities, such as counting, sequencing, and sorting, help develop pre-math skills. 160 pp.
WPH 0409

1•2•3 Science
Develop science skills—observing, estimating, predicting—using ordinary household objects. 160 pp.
WPH 0410

1•2•3 Games *No-Lose Games*
Foster creativity and decision-making with 70 no-lose games for a variety of young ages. 80 pp.
WPH 0402

1•2•3 Puppets
More than 50 simple puppets to make to delight children. 80 pp.
WPH 0404

TEACHING THEMES

BUSY BEES

For Two's and Three's

Day-by-day, hands-on projects and activities are just right for busy little ones.

Busy Bees–FALL
For fall fun and learning, these attention-getting activities include songs, rhymes, snacks, movements, art, and science projects. 136 pp.
WPH 2405

Busy Bees–WINTER
Enchant toddlers through winter with a wealth of seasonal ideas, from movement to art. 136 pp.
WPH 2406

Busy Bees–SPRING
More than 60 age-appropriate activities enhance learning for busy minds and bodies. 136 pp.
WPH 2407

Busy Bees–SUMMER
Encourage toddlers to build, develop, and explore with their senses and turn summer fun into learning. 136 pp.
WPH 2408

PLAY & LEARN

This creative, hands-on series explores the versatile play and learn opportunities of a familiar object. Perfect for working with young children ages 3 to 8. Each 64 pp.

Play & Learn with Photos
WPH 2303

Play & Learn with Magnets
WPH 2301

Play & Learn with Rubber Stamps
WPH 2302

CELEBRATIONS

Expand on your children's love for celebrations with these ideas for special learning fun.

Small World Celebrations
Multicultural Units • 160 pp.
WPH 0701

Special Day Celebrations
Nontraditional Units • 128 pp.
WPH 0702

Yankee Doodle Birthday Celebrations
Antibias Units • 128 pp.
WPH 0703

Great Big Holiday Celebrations
Traditional Units • 228 pp.
WPH 0704

THEME-A-SAURUS

Capture special teaching moments with instant theme ideas that cover around-the-curriculum activities.

Theme-A-Saurus
50 teaching themes—from Apples to Zebras—plus 600 fun and educational activity ideas. 280 pp.
WPH 1001

Theme-A-Saurus II
Sixty more teaching units—from Ants to Zippers—for hands-on learning experiences. 280 pp.
WPH 1002

Toddler Theme-A-Saurus
Sixty teaching themes combine safe, appropriate materials with creative activity ideas. 280 pp.
WPH 1003

Alphabet Theme-A-Saurus
From A to Z—26 giant letter recognition units filled with hands-on activities introduce young children to the *ABC's*. 280 pp.
WPH 1004

Nursery Rhyme Theme-A-Saurus
Capture the interest children have for nursery rhymes and extend it into learning. 160 pp.
WPH 1005

Storytime Theme-A-Saurus
Flannelboard patterns accompany 12 storytime favorites, plus hands-on activities and songs. 160 pp.
WPH 1006

EXPLORING SERIES

Environments

Selected environments become very real places in this book series that encourages exploration. Hands-on activities emphasize all the curriculum areas. Each book begins with the "known" and lets the curriculum expand as far as children's interests can stretch.

Exploring Sand and the Desert
WPH 1801

Exploring Water and the Ocean
WPH 1802

Exploring Wood and the Forest
WPH 1803

Instant Hands-on Ideas!

FREE sample newsletters available!

Totline® Newsletter and Super Snack News are perfect for working with young children because they are put together by the publisher of Totline® Books, a leader in early childhood resources for parents and teachers. Totline books and newsletters are guaranteed to be appropriate, enriching, and fun. Help your children feel good about themselves and their ability to learn by using the hands-on approach to active learning found in these two newsletters!

Warren Publishing House
P.O. Box 2250, Dept. Z, Everett, WA 98203

Totline® Newsletter

This newsletter offers creative hands-on activities that are designed to be challenging for children ages 2 to 6, yet easy for teachers and parents to do. Minimal preparation time is needed to make maximum use of common, inexpensive materials. Each bimonthly issue includes • seasonal fun • learning games • open-ended art • music and movement • language activities • science fun • reproducible teaching aids • reproducible parent-flyer pages and • Good Earth (environmental awareness) activities. *Totline Newsletter* is perfect for use with an antibias curriculum or to emphasize antibias values in a home environment.

Super Snack News

This newsletter is designed to be reproduced!

With each subscription you are permitted to make up to 200 copies per issue! They make great handouts to parents. Inside this monthly, four-page newsletter are healthy recipes and nutrition tips, plus related songs and activities for young children. Also provided are category guidelines for the CACFP reimbursement program. Sharing *Super Snack News* is a wonderful way to help promote quality childcare.

To receive your FREE copy of either Totline Newsletter or Super Snack News, call 1-800-773-7240.